All images and illustrations included in this book are in the public domain. Additional text and editing by Logan Thatcher.

Copyright © 2019 Ted Satterfield

All rights reserved.

ISBN-13: 9781700397478

CHRISTMAS GIFT SERIES

" I will close, hoping to be rewarded."

"I'm afraid to ask for more ..."

"We live at the Orphan's Home and are very glad that Christmas is coming."

"I will leave the back door unlocked."

"I will be a sweet girl and go to bed at 6 o'clock."

"If I don't spell all the words just right, next time I'll do better."

"This is the first letter I ever tried to write so please don't laugh at it."

A Note From the Editor

We didn't set out to make a book filled with letters to Santa — this book found us. During historical research over the last year for unrelated projects, we stumbled upon multiple newspapers from the first two decades of the 20th Century that compiled lists of letters to Santa, and after seeing so many adorable examples, we started setting them aside just for fun. As we continued to do our research, we kept finding charming examples and eventually had set aside enough for the creation of a book.

The following letters were lightly edited for spelling and punctuation whenever we felt minor changes would make them easier to read. Heavy editing wasn't necessary, and we assume the newspapers, or perhaps the parents or teachers, helped the children fix errors in their writing. In most instances, the letters are published in their original form in order to preserve the writer's voice. All of the letters bore publication dates old enough to assure they are in the public domain.

We hope this book gives you as much joy as it has given us.

Merry Christmas!

Logan Thatcher

Letters to Santa

Adorable Christmas letters from children over a hundred years ago

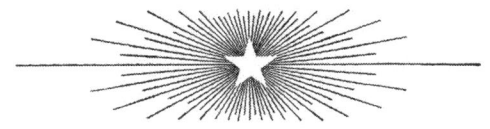

Can't always be good

Dear Santa Claus,

    I have tried to be good. You know I just cannot be good all the time. I want a nice big doll and a story book and a fur and muff and a dear little white kitten (I will take the best care of him, so you need not worry about him), and a dear little puppy and a pair of roller skates and I guess I cannot tell you any more things, for you know that I just can't spell them all.

    From yours truly,

    Sara

Newark, Delaware
1919

If there's no snow

Mr. Santa Claus,

    Sir, I must write and tell you what I want for Christmas. I guess we are going to have some snow pretty soon, but if we don't, I don't know what you are going to do. It is pretty muddy down this way and I guess you could not come with a sleigh and reindeer because you would sink through, and the little boys and girls would not know what became of you. I suppose you will have to get you a team of horses and a wagon. We are going to have a Christmas program in our schoolhouse, and I wish you would come too. We would thank you very much if you would. Well, I will say what I want for Christmas. I want a doll and lots of candy, peanuts and oranges.

    Yours truly,

    H. O. O.

Midway, Idaho
1903

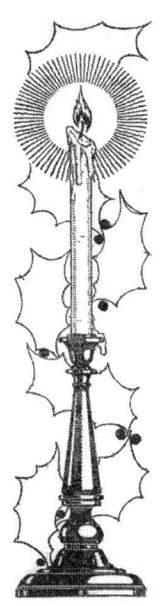

Not expecting presents

Dear Santa Claus,

    I thought I would ask you for some toys as I do not expect to get anything this Christmas. My father is dead, and my mother has to work for a living, for three of us children. I will ask you for a knife and a pair of knickerbockers corduroy pants. I must close now as it is getting late.

    Lloyd

Long Beach, California
1908

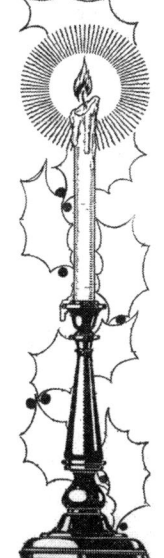

Chimney is full of soot

Dear Santa Claus,

    I am so glad Christmas is coming. I have tried to be a good boy, but I have done a few things I ought not to have done. Please bring my teacher Miss Montgomery a fountain pen. I don't believe you can come down my chimney because it is full of soot. I believe I want you to bring me a rifle. I think I will get an apple, an orange, and some fruit in my stocking. Please have Mrs. Santa Claus make us some candy. Please leave a lot for my sisters and brothers. Please remember all the little orphan children as they need more than us. I didn't think about Christmas being so near until mother told me about it the other day.

    Your friend,

    Tommie

__Starkville, Mississippi__
__1912__

Don't get burned

Dear Santa Claus,

    I will write and tell you what I want for Christmas. I want a bracelet, a doll's trunk, a story book and fireworks of all kinds, a few Roman candles, apples, oranges, raisins, pecans, peanuts and candy, dolls, piano and organ, a bugle and a little apron. I will put out the fire so you won't burn your feet.

    Mary

Chumuckla, Florida
1911

Sweet potatoes froze

Dear Santa Claus,

    I hope you will visit me this Christmas. I am a little girl eight years old. I am going to school. I have been very good and learn my lessons well. I want you to bring me a doll bed, a ring and locket. I suppose papa and mama will buy the rest that I want. Dear Santa, please take Grandma Swack a peck of sweet potatoes to make her a pudding, as her potatoes all froze. Take Grandpa a cap to keep his ears warm. Just take Aunt Minnie any old thing for she is easily pleased. Bring Grandpa and Grandma Andrews something too. If you pass through Montana, take Charlie something good to eat. He is living alone and has no cook, as I know of.

    Myrtle

               Foyil, Oklahoma
                     1914

Bring a monkey

Dear Santa Claus,

    I wish you would bring me a monkey, dolly, tablet and pencil, sled, automobile and horn, drum, set of dishes, red top boots, mittens, little engine, and candy, apples and nuts.

    Your good boy,

    Gail

Abilene Kansas
1912

Too expensive?

My Dear Santa,

I am going to tell you what I want and see if you will fill the bill for me. I know you will if it doesn't cost too much. I want a doll, a picture, doll bed, some fruit, some nuts. I will be glad to get anything that is nice. Please bring my baby sister lots of nice things. She is three years old. We are going to bed and will not watch for you, so you can come.

As ever yours,

Annie

Palestine, Texas
1908

4 lbs. of candy

Dear Santa Claus,

    I want a little white Teddy bear. I want two big dolls. Bring me a little story book. Bring me one box of candy and a little funny book. I want 4 lbs. of candy and 6 lbs. of oranges and 1 lbs. of nuts and two little penny dolls and I believe that is all for this Christmas.

    Goodbye, Santa Claus,

    Mildred

**Johnson City, Tennessee
1907**

Can you find us this year?

Dear Santie,

    I was afraid you would forget me this year for I have no papa to give you any money this year and mama says she is afraid Santa can't find us. This Christmas I would like a big doll and cradle. Bring me what you think I will like.

    Thank you,

    Vinita

                                       Ottumwa, Iowa
                                             1913

Please don't laugh, Santa

Dear Santa Claus,

This is the first letter I ever tried to write so please don't laugh at it. I am seven years old and in the second grade. I will not bother you much as I only want a big milk wagon with milk cans in it like the milk man has that brings us milk. Also, a nice warm sweater. Please bring me a pair of ball bearing skates and a new horn for my automobile. I would like lots of candy, nuts, oranges, grapes and apples.

Goodbye, dear Santa Claus.

From your friend,

Armond

Washington D.C.
1908

Living with the soldiers

Dear Santa Claus,

   I am a little boy from Chicago that is living with the soldiers at Fort Barrancas and I want you to come to see me at Christmas. My name is George, but they call me Pat because I am Irish. Please bring me a drum and some sticks and a pair of skates and a sled and a soldier's clothes with stripes on it and a train and choo-choo cars and some oranges and nuts and candy and please, Santa Claus, send my friend, also named George, some presents. Please don't forget me, because I am a good little boy.

   Pat

Pensacola, Florida
1910

There are four of us boys

Dear Old Santa Claus,

    I will now try and let you know that there are just four of us boys and I know it will be hard for you to think what would please us. So I will tell you what we want. Baby Paul can't write, so we have made it up that I must write for us all. Santa, Paul wants a rocking horse; Vernon, a drum and horn; Emmett wants a new suit of clothes, a drum and a horn; and I would like a magic lantern or a train of cars that will run on a track. We all want candy and nuts and fruit. I am 9 years old and Emmett is 7, Vernon is 5, and Paul is 3.

    Goodbye, old Santa. Remember us.

    Yours,

    Harold

Spokane, Washington
1903

The door's unlocked

Dear Santa Claus,

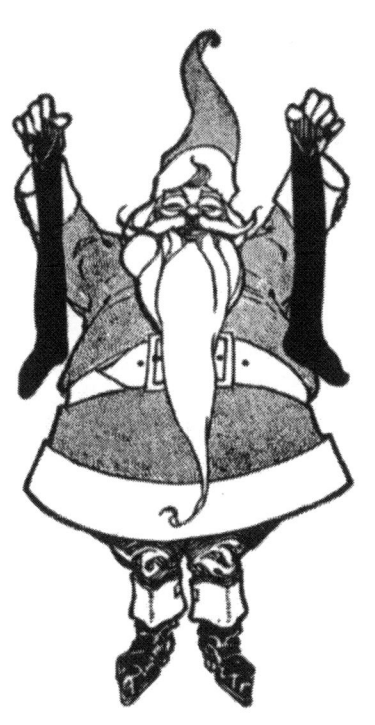

I want a stove and a kettle and a skillet to match the stove. I don't think you can get all these things, but I would like to have them. I want a doll worse than anything. I want a doll buggy and a little trunk. I want a girl's tricycle.

Don't wait to climb the roof. Just walk right in. The door is unlocked, and the nursery is on the right. Be sure to stop at my house as you go by in your automobile. I am 7 years old and I'm in second grade. I go to the Los Angeles seminary.

C. A.

Hermon, California
1908

Cloverport Santa is better

Dear Santa Claus,

    I am a little girl of six years old. Please do not forget to send me some candy, nuts, oranges, a little set of dishes, a table and a story book as I like to read. Do not forget papa and mama.

    I like the Santa at Cloverport better than the one at Decatur. He is better to me. I will be a nice little girl, so be sure to come.

    Gladys

Moweaqua, Illinois
1912

Sorry for any misspellings

Dear Santa Claus,

    I will write this letter to dear old Santa Claus. If I don't spell all the words just right, next time I'll do better. Santa Claus knows all the naughty things we do. I live out in the country and we have no happy times. If I just had one doll, I would remember you. We will have no Christmas tree in the valley where we live. And you can imagine how welcome a little present would be. Well, I'll close my letter now hoping to hear from you at Christmas time.

    Your friend,

    Gertrude

Weiser, Idaho
1902

Please don't forget us, Santa

Dearest Santa Claus,

    I want to write you a little letter to tell you what I and my little sister want. She is 3 years old, her name is Ethel, and she wants a big doll that will go to sleep and a doll cart, and I want an Irish mail wagon, or a big wagon and a cap pistol, caps and a pair of button shoes, and some candy and nuts too. I am 10 years old and go to school every day.

    Goodbye, dear Santa. Please don't forget us,

    Henry and Ethel

Beech Ridge, Illinois
1910

Asking for too much?

Dear Santa,

    Christmas is almost here, so I will tell you what I want before it is too late. I wish you would bring me a pair of skates, a sled, a ring, a locket and chain. I wish for many more things, but I am afraid if I ask for more you will not bring me any, but I will be pleased with what you do bring.

    I remain,

    Nellie

Batavia, Iowa
1909

Didn't come last year

Dear Mister Santa Claus,

    I am a little girl of 9 years. I have a papa, but he is never home. He does not buy me any toys. My mama works. I have a little sister 5 years old and 4 brothers, 2 younger than myself and 2 older. Last year Santa did not come and mama said I did not write him. Please, dear Santa, do not forget me and my little sister.

    Dollie

Seattle, Washington
1909

Landed a speaking part

Dear Santa Claus,

I will write and tell you what I want for Christmas. I want a blue coat, a pair of skates, a hat, a sled, a watch and some ribbons. I want some candy, nuts, bananas, oranges, figs and a box of oil colors. I am going to be on a Christmas program! I have a piece to speak.

Manila

Buxton, Louisiana
1910

I'd also like a gold ring

Dear Santa Claus,

    I thought I would write a few lines to tell you what I want. I want some candy and a toothbrush and a bracelet and my little brother Claude wants a rubber doll and some candy and a Teddy bear and a ball and I want a watch that runs and a doll and some oranges and bananas. My little sister Doris wants some candy and I want a gold ring. I go to school every day. I like my teacher very much. It is one-half mile to school. I will hang my stocking up Christmas Eve and don't forget papa and mama.

    Edna

Moravia, Iowa
1910

I think I'm a good boy

Dear Santa,

    I am a little boy 9 years old and live on a farm with my parents and have two sisters and two brothers. I go to school every day and I think I am a pretty good boy, so if you can bring me an air rifle with bb shots, some candy and oranges, I will be satisfied. Please remember my brothers and sisters and do not forget my uncle Jim.

    Joe

__Slater, Missouri__
__1910__

Please be quiet, Santa

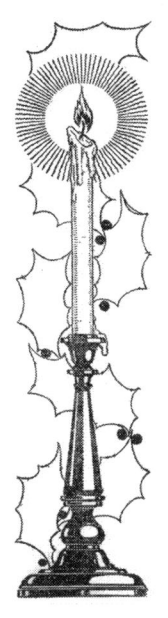

Dear Santa Claus,

    I thought I would write you a letter to let you know what I want for Christmas. I want a drum and a tin horn and that big Teddy bear in the Pike News stand and a sled to ride on and a doll with black hair and eyes.

    I will leave the back door unlocked. Santa, be quiet for my father and mother are very cross. Oh, Santa I forgot I want some candy, and nuts.

I am a good little boy,

    Frank

Clarksburg, West Virginia
1907

Watch out for the fire

Dear Santa Claus,

    I thought I would write you a few lines to let you know what I wanted you to bring me. I want a doll that will open and shut her eyes, and I want a buggy to ride her in, a set of dishes, a stove, and a story book, and a set of furs.

    Santa, be careful when you are coming down the chimney, for mama will have a fire in the fireplace. Please bring me some candy, nuts, oranges, figs, dates and bananas. Don't forget my sisters, they live on Woods Street. They did not say what they wanted.

From your friend,

Samuella

Nashville, Tennessee
1907

We'll go to bed early

Dear Santa Claus,

    I am a little girl 7 years old. I want you to bring me a metal head for my doll you gave me last Christmas. Please bring some dresses for her too and a cap. I have a little sister 10 months old, please bring her a rubber doll and a kitty. Her name is Ruth and she is awful sweet. Bring us some candy and nuts and all kinds of fruit and anything else you want to. We will go to bed early and be good.

    Your little girl,

    Forest

Prescott, Arkansas
1914

I reckon that's all

Hello Santa,

How are you this snowy winter? I am about to freeze. Santa, I want a doll buggy, a stove and a bed. Sister Ruby wants a doll bed, a doll and a set of dishes. So, this is all, I reckon.

Bessie and Ruby

Cookeville, Tennessee
1914

I'll be good until Christmas

Dear Santa Claus,

    I am a little boy. Please bring me a box of tools, a little gun, a horse and wagon, and don't forget my tree. Please fill my stockings. I will be a good boy until Christmas.

    Your friend,

    Carroll

Cambridge, Maryland
1913

Leave the rest at grandma's

Dear Santa Claus,

    Please bring me a devil-in-the-handbox, a train, cowboy suit, cowboy gloves, pistol, box of blanks, pistol case, story book, and a lot of good things to eat. I am a good boy and know my lessons every day. Now, Santa, leave the train at my home in Philadelphia. I will be there right after Christmas, but the other things I want you to leave me here at my grandma's.

    Yours with love,

    William

Philadelphia, Pennsylvania
1913

Remember the poor people

Dear Santa Claus,

    I am nine years of age. I live in sight of the school house and Miss Julia is my teacher. I am in the fourth grade. Dear Santa, I want a doll, a doll buggy, some toys, oranges, bananas, and a whole lot of nice things. Santa please don't forget me and don't forget the poor and pure in heart.

    Hoping you, dear Santa, have a merry Christmas.

Your little friend,

Bettie

Monroe, Arkansas
1912

Presents for five girls

Dear Santa Claus,

　　I am writing you to tell you what we all would like to have for Christmas. There are five of us girls and I am the oldest, and I am only 9 years. Then we have Maud, 6; Dolly, 5; Helen, 3; and Fannie, 1 1/2 years old. We all would like a doll and a picture book and if you could send a buggy or anything else we would be delighted. I don't want to ask for too much for I know you have a terrible lot of children to look after.

　　Hoping you will have a Joyous Christmas.

　　I am one of your children, …….

　　(Writer name was left blank)

Philadelphia, Pennsylvania
1915

Girl wants toys for boys

Dear Santa,

I am a seven-year-old girl and I want a cap gun and a fire engine. I know that these are toys for boys, but I hope you will give them to me even though I am a girl.

Dearest Old Santa,

Emily

**Lake Fremont, Minnesota
1914**

Don't know address

Dear Old Santa,

    I would like a lot of things but what I want most is a horse and farm for me to keep the horse. I think I have been good this year. I hope you don't have much trouble finding where I live. I can't remember my address but hopefully you can find the house.

    Robbie

Odenton, Maryland
1914

Just wants fireworks

Dear Santa,

    I have been a good little girl. I am 8 and I only want fireworks for Christmas. As much as you can fit on your sled.

    Laura

Dallas, Texas
1914

Always gets 100

Dear Santa,

I am five years old and go to school. I finished my first reader this week. I get 100 every Friday. I want a doll and a cart, a raincoat, a story book, and lots of good things to eat. Don't forget my twin sister, baby Virginia, mother and father.

Elizabeth

Chicago, Illinois
1914

Sled, wagon and drum

Dear Santa Claus,

    I like you very much and you are a good friend to me. How are you? I am well. And you will be glad to see me. I am living in Dyer and I have two sisters. I am going to school. I am nine years old and I am in the third reader. I want a sled and a wagon and a drum.

    Al

Dyer, Indiana
1910

Who is the president?

Dear Santa,

    I am trying to be a good boy, and I want you to bring me a lot of clothes, a scarf, a hat and some toys, please. I would also like to meet the President, but I cannot remember his name. I know George Washington is no longer the President.

    Willie

Norman, Oklahoma
1909

Remember the poor

Dear Santa Claus,

　　Will you please bring me a story book, a game, some candy and nuts, and some hair ribbons?

　　Don't forget the poor people.

　　Your friend,

　　Arlene

East Chicago, Indiana
1912

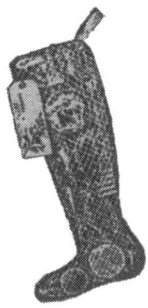

Don't forget me

Dear Santa Claus,

    I want you to bring me a mackintosh cape and a table that lets down on both sides and a set of dishes and a nice little box of writing papers and some little candy toys and I will hang up my stockings for all of these things and don't forget me and this is all of my letter for you.

    Goodbye, dear old Santa Claus,

    Alice

Newark, Delaware
1910

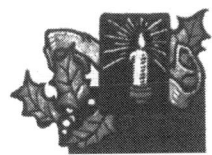

He sent money to Santa

Dear Old Santa Claus,

I am a little boy. I go to school every day. I am in the third grade. I will be promoted after Christmas to the fourth. Please bring me a little pistol, some candy, raisins, firecrackers, apples and some bananas.

I sent you some money. Did you get it? I put it in the mailbox. I will put some more in there for you. I also want some Roman candles and some oranges.

Well, goodbye, your good little boy,

Johnnie

Jefferson, Tennessee
1907

Boy wants an elephant

Dear Old Santa Claus,

    I have been a good boy all year, and I want you to bring me an airgun, a football, some marbles, a horn, an elephant, a cap pistol and some caps. I want you to bring me a hatchet and hammer and don't forget to bring me an automobile and I'd like to have a white stocking.

    I think that is all, so goodbye, old Santa.

From your little boy,

Whitfield

Arkansas
1905

Girl has been very good

Dear Santa Claus,

    I am a little girl ten years old. I am very good, and I go to school every day and I am very good so will you please bring me some Christmas presents. I want a doll, and a cab, and I want a doll bed, and I want a pair of shoes and stockings, and a stove, and some dishes and a pair of hair ribbons. I also want a red sled, and a Christmas Tree, and some candy and nuts and some oranges.

    Yours truly,

    Anna

South Bend, Indiana
1913

Bring bride doll

Dear Santa Claus,

I would like to have a toy watch, a bride doll, a bracelet for my doll, side combs and hair pins for the bride doll. Please bring candy, nuts and oranges. Please bring all the little folks nice things.

Your little friend,

Dorothy

Abilene, Kansas
1912

Papa will be away

Dear Santa Claus,

    I will write you a little letter. My name is Willie. I am four years old. My papa's name is Sam. He will not be with me on Christmas, as he is going to see grandpa and I don't want you to forget me. Santa, I want a horn and horse and a pistol and some caps to shoot with and some candy and oranges and bananas and nuts. That's all I can think of now. Hoping you will not forget my little sister, Hazel, and papa and mama.

    Good-bye, Santa Claus,

    Willie

Marshall, Missouri
1909

Bring Pearl everything

Dear Santa Claus,

    I will write a letter and tell you what I want for Christmas. I want a set of dishes and a black-headed doll and white-headed doll and an automobile and a doll carriage and a rocking chair and apples, oranges, nuts, and candy and everything you want to bring me.

    Your little girl,

    Pearl

Bluff City, Tennessee
1907

Box of chocolates

Dear Santa Claus,

I am going to write and tell you what I want. I want a bracelet, and a doll cart, and a handkerchief, and a box of chocolates. I go to Sunday school and school. My teacher's name is Verva. I like her fine. My studies are: Reading, arithmetic, history, language, geography, spelling, and writing. I have one sister and two brothers.

Please bring me what I want.

Your Loving Friend,

Nellie

Douds-Leando, Iowa
1913

Please don't leave me out

Dear Santa Claus,

    As Xmas Eve is drawing nigh and you will be slipping down the chimneys all over the land, I thought I would write and tell you not to leave me out this year. I am going to be a very good girl and am going to hang my stocking where you can get to it without much trouble. Now don't think just because I am writing to you dear Santa Claus that I want all the presents, but I want the other children to have just as many presents. Now then I guess I will close for this year and I hope to see you at our tree and joy shall speed the Xmas hours the whole night through.

    Yours truly,

    S. K.

Idaho
1903

Furs for me and doll

Dear Santa Claus,

I am six years old. I go to school and have one of the best teachers in the world. Her name is Miss McCallum. I want you to please bring me a set of furs for my doll, also a doll carriage. I would love to have a set of furs for myself too.

Mary

Hattiesburg, Mississippi
1908

Bicycle for long walk

Dear Santa Claus,

    As you will soon be here, I thought I would ask if you could bring me a bracelet, and I would like very much to have a bicycle, for I have quite a way to walk when I go to school. I am twelve years old now, and I hope you are as Jolly as when I was eleven. Would you please try to get me that nice doll at the store? I will be very careful with it if you can get it for me.

    Your friend,

    Lulu

Honolulu, Territory of Hawaii
1902

I'll go to bed early

Dear Santa Claus,

   Please come to see me Xmas and bring me a bugle, a rocking horse, a whole lot of firecrackers, candy, nuts, and all kind of fruit, and a harp and a rubber ball. Please come early. I will go to bed at seven o'clock and shut my eyes tight. I will not look. Indeed, I won't.

   Your little boy,

   Charlie

***Arkansas**
1910*

But once a year

Dear Santa Claus,

    I will now write you a nice little letter, for Christmas does not come but once a year and I do not write Santa Claus a letter but once a year. Now, well, I'll let you know I want a doll set for my dolls, a bedroom tea set, a bracelet, a ring, a sash pin, and that is all that I want, for I want you to give the poor little children something. But, Santa Claus, don't forget my brother Thomas who is four years old and my sisters Bessie and Jessie Mae.

    So, I will close. From your friend,

    Sadie

**Pensacola, Florida
1909**

She gets right to the point

Santa,

    Please bring me a little infant doll, and a box umbrella, and a sled, and a tin set of dishes and my stocking full of nuts and candy.

    Santa Claus, I love you, and send you a kiss.

    Goodbye,

    Kathryn

Newark, Delaware
1914

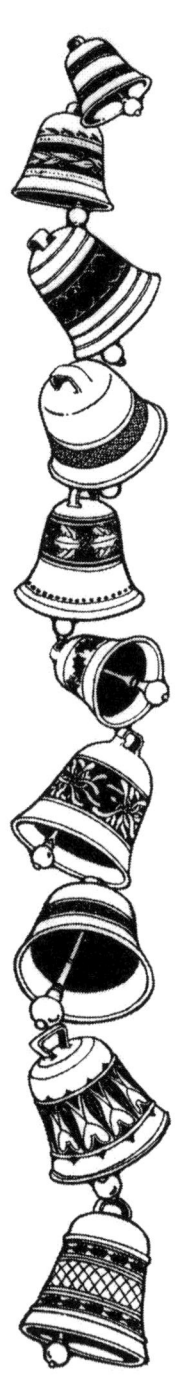

Trying to be good

Dear Santa Claus,

Bring me a cowboy's suit, cap pistol, hook and ladder wagon, fire department, football, magic lantern, new overcoat, hat, shoes, drum, game, horn, caps, large bag of marbles. Dear Santa, please bring me these things as I am trying to be a good boy. Hoping that you will remember to bring me what I have asked for in my letter.

I am yours, sincerely,

M. W.

Washington D.C.
1908

Shoe sizes, 5 and 11

Dear Santa Claus,

I will write you a few lines to tell you what I want for Christmas. I want a cap, some neckties, a pair of suspenders, a pair of shoes, size 5, and don't forget my sister. She wants a little iron bed and some little chairs, a table and a pair of shoes, size 11.

That will be all for this time.

John

Spokane, Washington
1903

Fallen on hard times

Dear Santa Claus,

Papa met with an accident in the city a little over a year ago. He fell from a building and hurt his head. Since then we have had so little that mama can't buy us any presents, because she makes so little. My brother wrote to ask you for a bicycle. A second hand one will do him. I want a pair of shoes and a pair of brown ribbons. Papa wants a warm woolen jacket.

Please Santa do not forget us, and we will thank you very much. My baby brother wants a little wagon.

Ruth

San Gabriel, California
1908

I promise not to peep

Dear Old Santa,

    I am a little boy and know all my letters and I thought I would write you a letter and tell you what I want you to bring me. Bring me a pistol, some caps, all kinds of nuts, candles, and I would like you to stop at Mr. Hardin's store and get me one of those climbing monkeys. Don't forget to bring little Eve a doll. And Grandpa lives with us, don't forget to bring him some nice things to eat. I will go to bed early and not peep.

    Your little boy,

    Alvin

__Kentucky__
__1912__

Did I ask for too much?

Dear Santa Claus,

    I am ten years old. This is the first year I ever went to school. Mama always taught me at home. I am in the fourth grade now. Now I want you to bring a story book, skates, ring and a sleeping doll and some candy and nuts. Dear Santa, do you think I have asked for too much? Santa, I want you to bring all I have asked for. Santa, I wish you Merry Christmas. Santa, I will hang my stocking up in the corner.

    Ina

Weiser, Idaho
1902

Bring fireworks

Dear Santa Claus,

    I am going to school this year and like to go very well. I want an airship, train, horn and a box of colors, and my brother John wants an automobile, horn, toy horse and wagon and any other toys that will do a boy his size. Don't forget to bring plenty of fireworks for us both.

    Frank

Pensacola, Florida
1910

Doll buggy and stove

Dear Santa Claus,

    I am a little girl and I go to Sunday School every Sunday. I will write and tell you what I want for Xmas. I want a doll and a little stove and a doll buggy and a doll bed, a set of candy and oranges and some nuts.

    Your friend,

    Ruby

Mounds, Illinois
1910

Your head will whirl

Dear Santa Claus,

I thought I would write and tell you what I want for Christmas. I thought I would write early so you would be sure to get my letter in time. It is almost three weeks till Christmas. I would like a Billiken doll, a book and a bracelet and a cup and saucer will do. I don't want much this year, some candies, nuts and dates; a pair of side combs, (the doll must have blue eyes and dark hair). I guess this won't be too much for you to bring, but dear me, how your head will have to whirl to get to every little girl's and boy's home. I hope there will be snow on the ground so you can come in your sleigh and drive the reindeer. I will have the front door unlocked so you can get in easier than to come down the chimney.

Belle

Floris, Iowa
1909

Won't ask for much this year

Dear Santa,

    I thought I would write and tell you what I want most for Christmas. Please bring me a go-cart for my Teddy Bear and the dolls you were so good to bring me last Christmas. I would like a new post card album, as I have my old one full. I guess that will be all. I won't ask for much, for you were so good to bring me so much last Christmas.

    Roxie

Granada, Minnesota
1909

Don't forget me

Dear Santa,

    I will write you a few lines to tell you where I live, my name and what I want for Christmas, so you will not forget me. I would like to have a story book or two, a ring, a bracelet, some candy and nuts. I guess this will be about as much as my share, for there are so many little boys and girls to give presents.

    I will close hoping you will not forget me.

    Bessie

Floris, Iowa
1909

Letter from an orphanage

Dear Santa,

    We live at the Orphan's Home and are very glad that Christmas is coming. It is such a happy, beautiful time. We want you to come and see us this Christmas. Violet wants a bracelet, some red hair ribbons, and a game. Ollie will love Santa Claus if he will bring her a ring, a red sweater and a toy bedroom set. Emma will be very happy if Santa will bring her a locket, a set of dishes and a hairbrush. Alice wants a pair of stockings, a long coat, a barrette and a cross. Helen wants a book and a watch. We are all very fond of candy and nuts.

    We remain your little friends,

Violet, age 12
Ollie, age 11
Emma, age 11
Alice
Helen

Ottumwa, Iowa
1909

Letter for a friend?

Dear Santa Claus,

This is a letter that I am writing for a little friend of mine to tell you what she wants you to bring her on Christmas Eve night. Her age is one year two months and her name is Olivia. She will be at 538 Meadow Street and will hang up a little bag and go to sleep hoping that you will come and see her on that night. Dear Santa, this is what little Olive wants you to bring her on Christmas Eve night: A little red cap, red silk ribbon, two dresses, one doll, oranges, nuts, cake, candy, apples, baby ring, a set of dishes, a book, a baby shawl, earrings, necklace, a Teddy bear, a little bracelet, two little woolen shirts, a set of baby furs, two little under skirts and a little baby buggy blanket.

(Anonymous)

1910

Out in the country

Dear Santa Claus,

    I am a little girl eight years old and live in the country nine miles north of Slater and go to the Davis school. Mr. Sullivan is my teacher. I will now tell you what I want for Christmas. I would like to have a doll, a story book, a doll cradle, and a ring, and some candy. And bring my little sister Oretha who is four years old something nice. Remember all the poor little girls and boys with something nice.

    Lorena

Slater, Missouri
1910

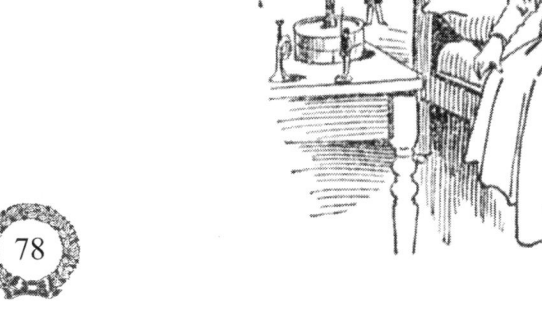

I'll be a sweet girl

Dear Santa Claus,

I am a little girl, and I want you to please bring me a doll, a stove, a piano and some candy, nuts, oranges, raisins, figs and apples. I will be a sweet girl and go to bed at 6 o'clock. Santa, please don't forget my papa; he wants a black silk muffler.

Earline

Nashville, Tennessee
1907

Remember the orphans

Dear Santa Claus,

    Will you find me a doll, a bed, little wagon, lots of nuts and candy? Don't forget my sister, Barbara. She wants a great big doll and lots of nuts and candy.

    Don't forget the little orphans.

    Your little friend,

    Jessie

Birmingham, Alabama
1910

Bring some checkers

Dear Santa Claus,

I am a little boy 9 years old. Please bring me a tool box and an air gun and bring me a train on a round track. Please bring me a football and a little wagon. And a little football suit, a story book and some checkers. Please do not forget the poor people. I want all kinds of fireworks. Al says that he wants a drum and all kinds of fruits.

Your little friend,

Gann

Prescott, Arkansas
1914

Hope to see you

Dear Santa Claus,

I want you to bring me some fireworks of all sorts. I want a tricycle, a little train with four coaches and a track 36 inches long like a horseshoe, and a toy railroad lantern. I want some nuts and fruits of all kinds, and anything you think will be nice for a little boy like I am. I will close with saying I hope to see you at Christmas. I am a little boy 5 years old.

J. I.

**Double Springs, Tennessee
1914**

Bring a coconut

Dear Santa Claus,

Please bring me some candy, bananas, oranges, a dog, a horse, a doll and a coconut. I am 9 years old and am in the first grade.

Your little friend,

Harrison

Monroe, Arkansas
1912

Hoping for reward

My dear Santa,

How are you getting along these cold days? I hope it won't be too cold for you to come to see me this Xmas. Santa, I want you to bring me a doll and anything that you want me to have. I will be pleased with anything. I am a little girl with dark hair, blue eyes, fair complexion, and about 4 feet tall. Santa, I am writing because I want your doll. I have seen the doll that you have been giving and think it is the prettiest thing I ever saw. Well, I will close, hoping to be rewarded.

Your little friend,

Bessie

Cabot, Arkansas
1912

Willing to share

Dear Santa Claus,

    As it is about time for you to visit me again, I will tell you what I want. I want a raincoat and hat, an air gun, a rubber tire hand car, a drum, lots of fireworks, some candy and fruits. Now, Santa, if you think this is too much for one little boy, I will share part of my Xmas with the poor little starving little children in Belgium.

    I am, as ever, your little boy,

    Francis

Irvington, Kentucky
1914

A whole bushel of love

My Dear Old Santa,

    I'll write you a few lines to let you know what I want for Christmas. Now, Santa, there are a great many things I would like to have. You are such a dear old fellow, and I do not like to impose on you, as you have so many boys and girls to remember. I will only ask you to bring me a doll and a sleigh, and don't forget my dear little friend, Mabel, in Buffalo, New York. Oh, dear old Santa, if you were only here I would love you a whole bushel. Cheer up, dear old Santa, it will soon be Xmas and I will be glad.

    Now goodbye until I see you.

    I remain your friend,

    Marion

Hammond, Indiana
1910

Bring aunt to me

Dear Santa Claus,

    I am a little girl 7 years old. Please bring me a doll, some nuts and fruit. And if you find my dear Aunt Nora in your round, just put her in your pack and bring her to me. I would like her best of all this year.

    Thelma

Ardmore, Oklahoma
1909

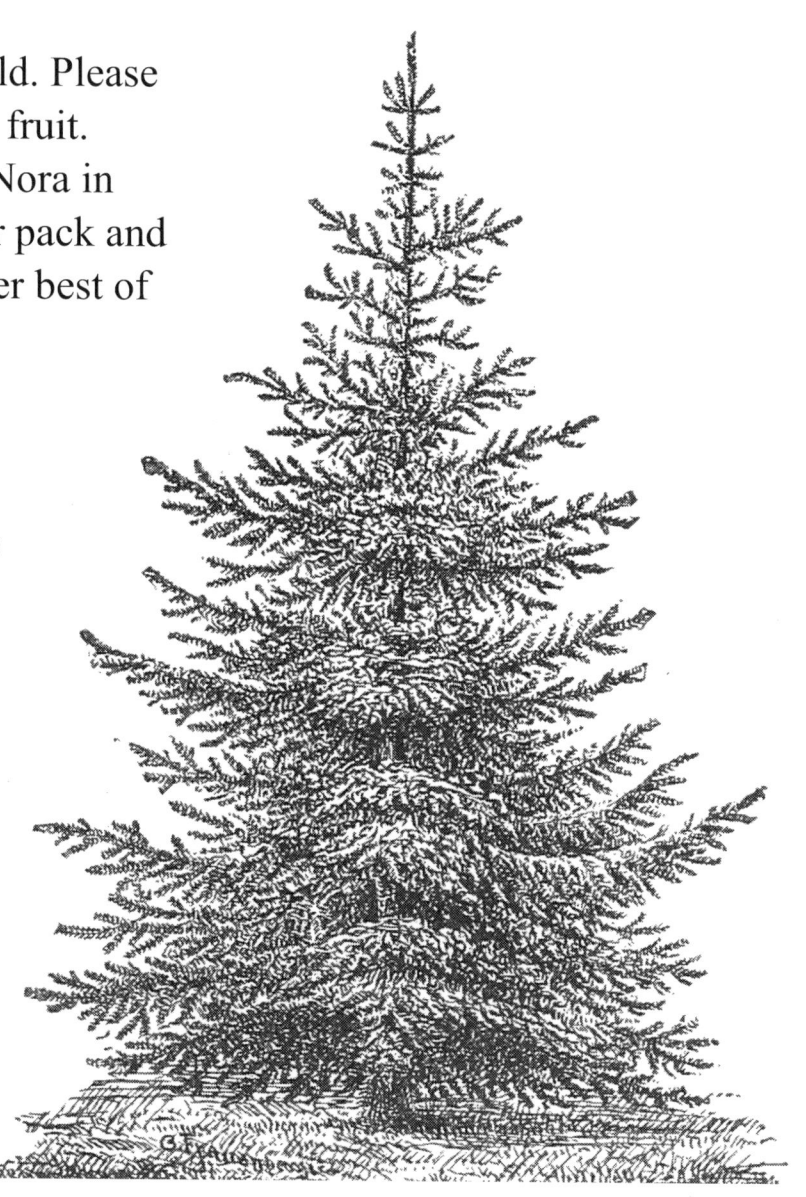

Brother is naughty

Dear Santa Claus,

I want so many things for Christmas I scarcely know how to tell you. I want a doll carriage, a pair of skates, a three-foot-doll, a doll trunk, as many nice books as you can spare. Please don't bring less than six.

Don't forget my brother Gene. He is naughty, but bring him a little something.

Gladys

Gary, Indiana
1912

Hope you never die

Dear Santa,

    I guess you are going to visit us again this Xmas. I want you to bring me a wagon, a baseball and bat, a set of small tools and a little knife. I want you to bring my little baby sister a nice doll and please have your mama to dress it real sweet. Bring her a china-tea set, and some nice fruits for her to eat.

    My dear Santa, I hope you will never die.

    Adele

Clover, South Carolina
1909

A dog and a cat

Dear Santa Claus,

    I want you to bring me a talking and walking doll. I want a doll buggy and a dog and a cat. I want a large set of play dishes. I want a little bed for my doll and a little swing for my doll. I want a little broom and a play watch. Please bring them dear Santa Claus.

    Your little friend,

    L. V.

Corvallis, Oregon
1907

Time is running out

Dear Santa Claus,

    I am a little girl eight years old. As the time is fast approaching for you to distribute your good things, I don't want you to forget me. I want you to please bring me a tricycle, a pair of rubber shoes and some of the good things you have to eat, such as candy, oranges and apples. Please don't forget my little sister.

    Your little girl,

    Judith

Boer, Virginia
1909

Don't forget anyone

Dear Santa Claus,

I am a little boy five years old and I would like for you to bring me a dolly that opens and shuts its eyes, a doll buggy to wheel it in, a toy train and a football to play. Now, dear Santa, you don't want to forget any of the little boys and girls.

Your friend,

Edward

Chapman, Kansas
1912

Papa is the foreman

Dear Santa Claus,

    I will write you a letter. I am a little boy and I go to school. I live here in Wellington but would rather be in Marshall where you came to see me last Christmas. My papa is section foreman and his name is J. F.

    Santa, please bring me a watch and chain and some candy and I want lots of toys. Don't forget my three brothers. Their names are Clarence, Kirtley and Joseph, and don't forget my little cousin Mary. She lives at Marshall. This is my first letter to you so I will close.

Your little friend,

Willie

Wellington, Missouri
1909

Is that a problem?

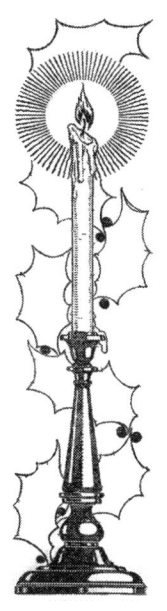

Dear Santa Claus,

    I am going to write and tell you what I want. I want a doll cart, and a red handkerchief, and a box of candies. I go to Sunday School every week. I have one sister and two brothers. My family does not have a chimney. I hope that's not a problem for you. Well, I will close. Please bring me Santa what I want.

    Your loving friend,

    Susan

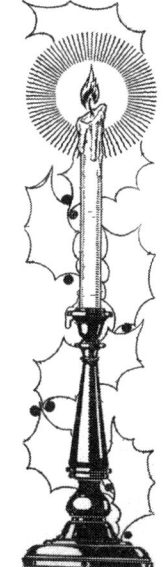

Lincoln, Nebraska
1913

Biggest doll you have

Dear Santa Claus,

    I thought I would write you a letter to tell you the things I want for Christmas. These are the things I want: a doll with flaxen hair and blue eyes, the biggest one you have. I want the doll to have on a white silk dress. Besides that, I want a ring; a pretty gold one with a pearl set in it. I hope that I am not asking for too many things but do please bring me some candy and nuts. I am almost through my letter, but a few more things: I would like to see you dear old Santa Claus. I want you to come Christmas night. I guess I will close my letter now, but I do wish Christmas would hurry up and come. Goodbye till next year.

    Hoping you will send me the things I ask for,

    M.D.

Caldwell, Idaho
1903

First year at school

Dear Santa Claus,

I am a little girl six years old. This is my first year at school and I am doing fine, although I was sick and had to lose four weeks. I would like for you to bring me a nice rocking chair and a big round table and a small stool and doll and an automobile and a few fireworks, some fruit and chocolate candy for I like it very much.

Wishing you a very Merry Christmas!

I am sincerely your little friend,

Annie

Pensacola, Florida
1909

You are very kind to the poor

Dear Santa Claus,

    I read that you were going to give away toys on Christmas day. I think that you are very kind. I am a poor girl. My father does not have much work. I have a little brother about 5 years old. He said he would like to have a coat for Christmas. I would like a coat and a pair of rubbers. I wear No. 3 shoes. I think that you are very kind to the poor.

    God will bless you,

    Marguerite

Los Angeles, California
1908

Boy's mama has a request, too

Dear Santa Claus,

    Here comes a little 7-year-old boy to tell you what he wants for Christmas. Please bring me an air gun (one that will shoot a sure enough shot), a sled so I can coast down the hill with my little sister, a little drum, some nice candy, oranges, nuts, apples, cake, and please, dear Santa, don't forget to bring my little sister a doll baby. She is too small to write you a letter. If you don't have enough for both stockings, please put all in hers.

    So goodbye, dear Santa, until Christmas.

    Your little friend,

    Maurice

    P. S. Mama says don't forget to bring a bottle of Castor oil.

Welser, Idaho
1902

We hope you've enjoyed your copy of "Letters to Santa." Hopefully this book has helped enhance your Christmas spirit and worked to grow the love between you and the very special people in your life.

Made in the USA
Columbia, SC
12 December 2021